W9-CII-980

CHRIS **KYLE**

American Sniper

CHRIS **KYLE**

American Sniper

BY ALEXIS BURLING

CONTENT CONSULTANT
BOB SEALS
US ARMY SPECIAL FORCES, RETIRED
RAEFORD, NORTH CAROLINA

Essential Library
An Imprint of Abdo Publishing | abdopublishing.com

abdopublishing.com

Published by Abdo Publishing, a division of ABDO, PO Box 398166, Minneapolis, Minnesota 55439. Copyright © 2016 by Abdo Consulting Group, Inc. International copyrights reserved in all countries. No part of this book may be reproduced in any form without written permission from the publisher. Essential Library™ is a trademark and logo of Abdo Publishing.

Printed in the United States of America, North Mankato, Minnesota
062015
092015

Cover Photo: Paul Moseley/The Fort Worth Star-Telegram/AP Images
Interior Photos: Paul Moseley/The Fort Worth Star-Telegram/AP Images, 1, 6; Richard W. Rodriguez/The Fort Worth Star-Telegram/AP Images, 9; Erath County Sheriff's Office/AP Images, 13; Seth Poppel/Yearbook Library, 14, 17, 18; Mass Communication Specialist 2nd Class Shauntae Hinkle-Lymas/US Navy, 22; Chief Mass Communication Specialist John Lill/US Navy, 24; Mass Communication Specialist 2nd Class Trevor Welsh/US Navy, 28; Mass Communication Specialist 2nd Class Kyle D. Gahlau/ US Navy, 31; US Navy, 33; RW/MediaPunch/IPX/AP Images, 34; Dan Howell/ Shutterstock Images, 38; Paul Moseley/Fort Worth Star-Telegram/MCT/Getty Images, 41, 64, 85; Maurizio Gambarini/Picture-Alliance/DPA/AP Images, 44; Chris Haston/ NBC/NBCU Photo Bank/Getty Images, 47; Sebastien Micke/Contour/Getty Images, 50, 62, 69, 71; Trae Patton/NBC/NBCU Photo Bank/Getty Images, 54; Red Line Editorial, 57; Tyler Golden/NBC/NBCU Photo Bank/Getty Images, 61; PN2/PNP/ WENN/Newscom, 67; Trae Patton/NBC/NBCU Photo Bank/Getty Images, 75; Warfighters Foundation/Splash/Splash News/Corbis, 76; Larry W. Smith/EPA/Corbis, 80; EPA European Pressphoto Agency b.v./Alamy, 83; Cpl. Damien Gutierrez, 86; Atlaspix/Alamy, 89; Tyler Golden/NBC/Getty Images, 94

Editor: Mirella Miller
Series Designer: Becky Daum

Library of Congress Control Number: 2015934084

Cataloging-in-Publication Data

Burling, Alexis.
  Chris Kyle: American sniper / Alexis Burling.
    p. cm. -- (Essential lives)
Includes bibliographical references and index.
ISBN 978-1-62403-893-8
1. Kyle, Chris, 1974-2013--Juvenile literature. 2. Iraq War, 2003-2011--Juvenile literature. 3. Snipers--United States--Biography--Juvenile literature. 4. United States. Navy.SEALs--Biography--Juvenile literature. I. Title.
359--dc23
[B]   2015934084

CONTENTS

CHAPTER
ONE

SHOTS FIRED

It was a brisk, sunny morning on January 25, 2013. Thirty-eight-year-old former Navy Special Operations SEAL (SEa, Air, Land) sniper Chris Kyle kissed his eight-year-old son, Colton, and six-year-old daughter, McKenna, before dropping them off at school. As he hopped back into his black Ford F-350 truck and started driving toward his home in Midlothian, Texas, a suburb of Dallas, a woman approached his truck and motioned for him to roll down the window.

Introducing herself as Jodi Routh, a special education aid at his children's elementary school, the woman told Kyle she had been hoping to speak to him about her son, Eddie Ray. Eddie Ray Routh was 25 years old, an ex-marine, and deeply troubled. According to Jodi, for the past three years since leaving active duty, Eddie Ray had not been able to hold down a job. Instead, he had cycled in and out of emergency rooms, mental hospitals, and even jail cells because of his violent behavior. A doctor had prescribed psychiatric drugs to lessen his

Chris Kyle had no idea his work helping veterans would affect his and his family's life so drastically.

paranoia, but none seemed to be working. Jodi told Kyle she was constantly worried Eddie Ray would harm himself or, worse, others.

Kyle was used to these kinds of requests from war veterans' distressed family members. Since he had returned to Texas after his fourth and last tour in Iraq in 2009, after a decade of service, Kyle had made it his mission to help veterans who were suffering from stress or exhibiting suicidal tendencies. Sometimes he pushed them to get back in shape by teaching them rigorous exercise routines similar to ones they learned in the military. Other times, he treated them to a day at the nearby shooting range so they could blow off steam. Kyle reassured Jodi he would do whatever it took to help her son get back on track.

A Fatal Mistake

One week later on Saturday, February 2, Kyle and his wife, Taya, took Colton to his ball game. After the game, Kyle's

"I was so happy that somebody was listening . . . and willing to help. [Kyle] wanted to help Eddie . . . [He] knew from what I told him that my kid was suffering . . . and he knew it was hurting me. That was the first time in a long time that I had felt a little sense of relief. I felt some hope for Eddie, that it wasn't just going to be bad for him, and that maybe something good was gonna happen."[1]
—Jodi Routh, in an interview with the New Yorker magazine

Kyle frequented Rough Creek Lodge's rifle range
either alone or with veterans he was helping.

neighborhood friend, Chad Littlefield, dropped by the
Kyles' house and the two men packed the F-350 truck
with rifles, gear, and snacks. Then they headed over to
pick up Routh for an afternoon of target practice.

When Kyle and Littlefield arrived, Routh was already
in a bad mood. He had just gotten in a fight with his
girlfriend Jen, to whom he had proposed marriage the
night before. Despite Routh's noticeable agitation, Kyle
assured him a bit of fresh air and the hour-long drive
through the Texas countryside to Rough Creek Lodge
and its 1,000-yard (910 m) rifle range would do him a
world of good.

At approximately 3:00 p.m., the men arrived at their
destination. Kyle and Littlefield went inside the main

building to register while Routh stayed behind in the truck. A few minutes later, a Rough Creek employee radioed a request to unlock the metal gate that protected the rest of the grounds. Kyle drove the short distance down a dirt road to the private shooting platform and raised a red flag to let everyone else on the property know a shooting session was in progress. If all went according to plan, Kyle, Littlefield, and Routh would be spending the next hour aiming their guns at targets and hopefully working through some of Routh's problems in the process.

But all did not go according to plan. At 4:55 p.m., nearly one full hour after Kyle and his crew were scheduled to finish shooting, the red flag was still flapping in the wind. Sensing something fishy, a Rough Creek wilderness guide named Justin Nabours drove to the site to determine why the group had gone over their reserved time limit. What he found shocked him to his core. Littlefield was lying on his back with seven gunshot wounds to the chest. Next to him, a few feet away, was Kyle—face down in a pool of blood seeping from his back and head. Though Nabours called 911 immediately and tried to do cardiopulmonary resuscitation (CPR) on the bodies, his efforts did no good. Both men were dead.

A Murder That Shocked the Nation

Immediately following the murder, friends, family members, news reporters, military personnel, fellow Texans, and strangers from throughout the country struggled to piece together what happened on that fateful February afternoon. Who killed Kyle and Littlefield? And why?

Because no security cameras were on the site, an exact picture of what transpired could not be known. But in the weeks and months that followed, gruesome evidence began surfacing. Kyle and Littlefield were not killed by a flurry of stray bullets from a neighboring platform. A maniacal stranger did not execute the men on a random shooting spree. No, it

A TELLING TEXT MESSAGE

Kyle dedicated much of his post–Navy SEAL life to helping war veterans deal with their demons. He had wrestled with his own problems after four tours of duty in Iraq. Perhaps this is why he was concerned about Routh's mental state the day they went shooting. In a text message sent to Littlefield a short time before they were both killed, Kyle referenced Routh who was sitting in the back seat of the truck: "This dude is straight-up nuts."[2] Littlefield responded telling Kyle to watch his back. Unfortunately, it was too late.

was Routh who pulled the trigger, murdering Kyle and Littlefield at close-point range.

Routh would eventually be arrested for what he had done. A lengthy investigation into his motives—and the state of his sanity—would take place in the years to come. And in February 2015, he would stand trial for his crimes. But for now, the world would focus on mourning the loss of one of the most legendary sharpshooters in US military history. Chris Kyle was gone, but he would never be forgotten.

"THESE KILLINGS WERE BRUTAL"

Located on a hill overlooking 11,140 acres (4,510 ha) of remote, undisturbed prairie, the Rough Creek Lodge and Resort is a posh—and exclusive—place to be.[3] Kyle frequently used the resort's shooting range. Thanks to his celebrity status as the US Navy SEAL's best sniper, he was allowed to come and go on the property as he pleased. And because he was such a practiced sharpshooter, he did not goof around during target practice. He always treated the weapons he used with caution and respect. Kyle had never given the lodge's guards cause to worry. So they were shocked to learn of his murder on their property—particularly Danny Briley, the first Texas Ranger to arrive at the scene after Kyle and Littlefield's bodies were discovered. "This was a brutal killing," Briley told the jury during Routh's trial in February 2015. "There was no question that I was dealing with someone very violent. . . . You can't accidentally shoot someone that many times."[4]

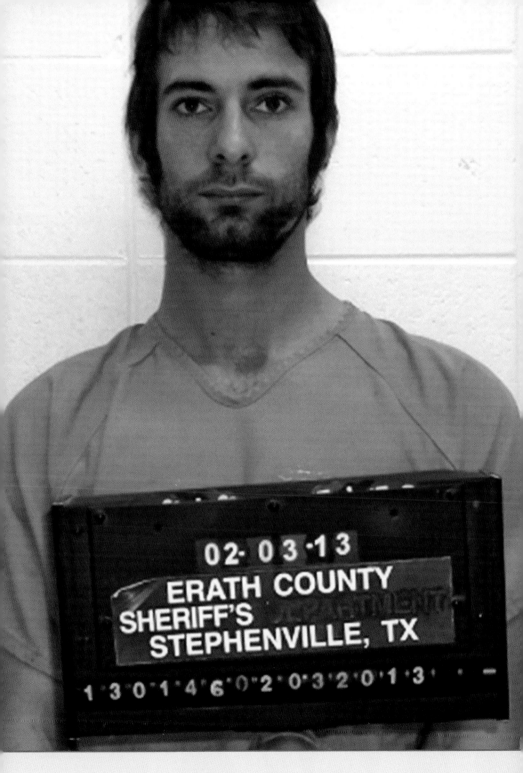

Routh's mug shot on February 3, 2013

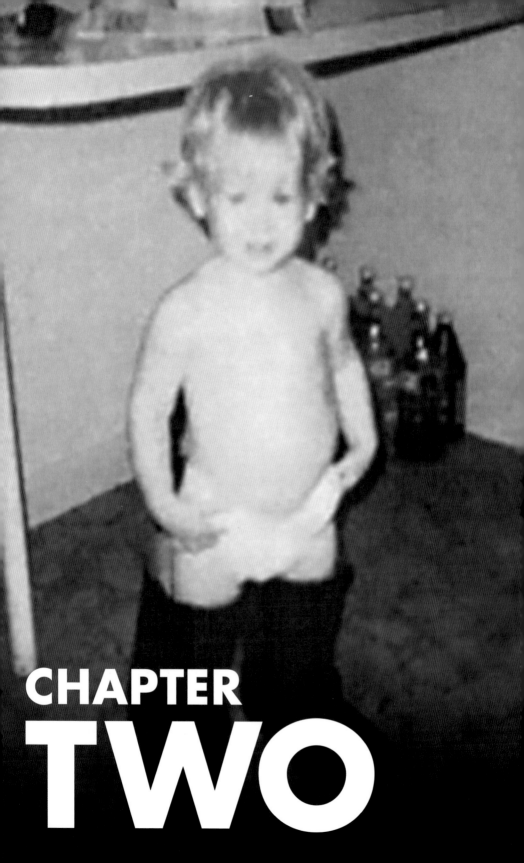

CHAPTER
TWO

A TEXAS COWBOY

C hristopher Scott Kyle was born on April 8, 1974, in Odessa, Texas, to parents Deby and Wayne. Deby taught Sunday school and worked at a juvenile detention center when Chris and his younger brother, Jeff, were in school. Wayne was a manager at Southwestern Bell/AT&T and volunteered as a deacon at the local church.

The Kyles went to church every Sunday morning and Wednesday evening. Of the four of them, Chris and his father were particularly close. "In a lot of ways my father was my best friend growing up," Chris wrote in his 2012 autobiography, *American Sniper*. "He was able at the same time to combine that [treating me like a friend] with a good dose of fatherly discipline."[1]

When Chris was in elementary school, his father's job moved the family to Midlothian, a suburb of Dallas 30 minutes away by car. It was there Chris first discovered his lifelong love of guns. As soon as he was old enough to obtain a shooting license, he learned how

Chris grew up in a tight-knit Christian family in Texas.

to hunt deer, wild turkeys, and small game animals such as rabbits and squirrels. When he was seven or eight years old, his father gave him his first rifle.

Ride 'em Bronco!

As a teenager, Chris had a knack for hunting. Chris admired animals, particularly cattle and horses. He raised steers and heifers for Future Farmers of America, an organization dedicated to teaching kids about agriculture and breeding healthy livestock. Sometimes he won prizes at county fairs for best-groomed cow in the barn. Chris's real passion, though, was rodeo. When he was around 16 years old, he started riding bulls, but soon he switched to horses after he fell off a bull one too many times. Before long, saddle bronc riding became his specialty. In his beat-up cowboy boots and dusty Wrangler jeans, Chris would squeeze his thighs onto the horse's sides, let the rest of his body go loose, and whoop and holler for

Along with working with animals, Chris also enjoyed playing sports, such as football.

eight seconds as the horse bucked upward and sideways, trying to shake Chris from its back.

By the time Chris graduated from Midlothian High School in 1992 and started his first year at Tarleton State University in Stephenville, Texas, he was picking up shiny first-place belt buckles and winning rodeo competitions throughout the state. Then tragedy struck. At the end of his freshman year, in 1993, a bronco

After high school, Chris continued pursuing his dreams of competing in rodeo competitions.

flipped over on him in the chute during an event, pinning him to the ground. The fallen horse kicked and struggled so much on top of Chris that it knocked the young man unconscious.

When Chris woke up in the hospital, he was in a world of pain—broken ribs, a dislocated shoulder, and bruised lungs and kidneys. He even had pins in his wrists with screws that stuck out of his skin to hold his bones together! Luckily, he did not die from his injuries. But they were so severe that doctors said it would take time—months, if not years—for him to recover. Whether Chris liked it or not, his rodeo career was over.

A New Career Path

During Chris's first year at Tarleton State, when he was not on the road hunting down rodeo competitions before his accident, he kept himself busy by learning the ropes of his second passion: ranching. When he was not in class, Chris lived and worked as a hired hand on a 10,000-acre (4,000 ha) ranch in Hood County for extra spending money. He made $400 per month planting wheat and doling out feed to the cattle. Later he trained horses that helped keep the cows in line.

"Working on a ranch is heaven," Chris wrote of his

TIGHT QUARTERS

Chris adored ranching. But as a ranch hand, his living quarters were anything but comfortable. He slept in a cramped bunkhouse barely big enough to fit a single bed. He hung his belongings on a pole in the corner of the room. In the winter, he slept wearing all of his clothes to keep from catching a chill. "The worst thing about it was the fact that there wasn't a proper foundation under the floorboards," Chris wrote in his memoir. "I was continually doing battle with raccoons and armadillos, who'd burrow in right under my bed."[3]

time on rancher David Landrum's farm. "It's a hard life, featuring plenty of hard work, and yet at the same time it's an easy life. You're outside all the time. Most days it's just you and the animals. You don't have to deal with people or offices . . . you just do your job."[4]

Despite his love of the land, Chris began to feel something was missing in his life—particularly after he no longer had the thrill of rodeo to keep him energized. He had never been much of a student and was growing bored in his classes. Plus he had always been curious about joining the military before his parents convinced him to first get an education. So at the end of his second year in college, in 1994, Chris dropped out of school so he could follow his dream. "Since that [joining the military] was what I really wanted to do, there was no sense waiting," he wrote in his memoir.[5] But first, he needed to train.

Early Disappointment

After more than one year of training by ranching full-time and constant exercise and preparation on the side, Chris was ready to join the military. On the day he went to the recruiting station in 1996, he was confronted with a range of options. Did he want to fly jet planes for the air force? Attack targets and jump out of airplanes as an Army Ranger? Be a part of on-the-ground forces as a marine? Which one was right for him? After careful consideration and a particularly persuasive sales pitch by the navy recruitment officer, Chris decided it was his destiny to become a US Navy SEAL. To do that, he needed to quickly enroll in the Basic Underwater Demolition/Scuba (BUD/S) preliminary training course. "When I heard how hard

SIGN ME UP, UNCLE SAM!

Joining the military is never an easy decision. Even after the initial choice has been made, an enlistee can take many paths: the air force, the army, the coast guard, the marines, and the navy. But first there are a few rules:

All military hopefuls must be US citizens or resident aliens (foreigners who are permanent US residents but do not have citizenship). They must also be at least 17 years of age and have a high school diploma. Those who wish to become officers are required to have a college degree.

More often than not, there are weight and height requirements, too. A 5-foot (1.5 m), 18-year-old woman who wants to join the US Army, for example, must weigh at least 97 pounds (44 kg) and no more than 128 pounds (58 kg), whereas a 6-foot (1.8 m) man of the same age must weigh at least 140 pounds (64 kg) and no more than 190 pounds (86 kg).[6]

Plenty of medical conditions, such as a history of asthma, thyroid disorders, or physical disfigurements such as the absence of a thumb, can also knock a recruit out of the running. Even if enlistees are perfectly healthy on the surface, they must pass a physical examination before being allowed to advance.

The US military requires all potential soldiers to take written exams to prove their skills. Similar to school, failing or low scores are not tolerated.

One of the physical training exercises in the BUD/S training course involves moving a 600-pound (270 kg) log.

it was, how the instructors ran you and how less than 10 percent of the class would qualify to move on, I was impressed," Chris said. "Just to make it through the training, you had to be one tough [dude]. I liked that kind of challenge."[7]

But it would be a long while before Chris's dream would be realized. During a routine physical examination required for all potential recruits, he was disqualified because of the pins in his wrists. He begged the doctors to write him an excuse. He pleaded with navy officials to make an exception and overlook his injuries. But no one would budge. Instead, Chris resigned himself to following his second-choice career path once again: becoming a rancher.

For the next three years, Chris worked odd jobs on ranches throughout the western half of the United States. But just before he left Colorado to return to Landrum's ranch in Texas, something unexpected happened. As he states in his memoir, Chris received a phone call that would change the course of his life. It was a navy recruiter. He was calling to ask Chris to become a SEAL.

CHAPTER
THREE

TRAINING TO BECOME A HERO

"Drop! One hundred push-ups! NOW!" commanded a BUD/S instructor as dozens of exhausted and sweaty Navy SEAL hopefuls threw themselves on the floor for what seemed like the millionth time that hour.[1] Only a few months prior, in February 1999, Kyle had been enrolled in mandatory basic training for navy sailors. But after weeks of sitting around, gaining weight, and not enough physical activity, Kyle had decided he was ready for a change. "[Navy] boot camp is designed to prepare you to sit on a ship . . . I wanted something more . . . a physical challenge," Kyle said.[2]

As soon as there was an open spot, Kyle dropped out of navy boot camp and switched to BUD/S, a training course held at the Naval Special Warfare Training Center in Coronado, California. It was a six-month commitment, including five weeks of teaching, to

Special Warfare Training provides more challenges than regular navy boot camp.

include basic physical and mental preparation for the rigorous training to follow. Three stages of instruction followed: eight weeks of physical conditioning, eight weeks of diving, and nine weeks of land warfare—patrolling, demolition, marksmanship, basic weaponry, and land navigation.

Kyle had heard plenty of horror stories from people who had gone through BUD/S before; he knew it was brutal. It included relentless drills at all hours of the day and night. Training schedules allowed barely any sleep—sometimes fewer than four hours. And he could get kicked out of the program any time for failing to finish an exercise. "Essentially, the instructors beat you

SPECIAL OPS

Each arm of the US military is designed to perform specific tasks. Some smaller groups are more specialized and require more training hours. US Special Operations Forces consist of several distinct and highly capable forces within the US Armed Forces. The Army Special Forces, commonly known as Green Berets, specialize in training and assisting friendly troops from other nations throughout the globe. The Army Rangers are more of a direct assault force; they take down targets with surgical precision. Members of Air Force Special Operations provide or control air support, establish airfields, and rescue downed pilots or aircrew from battle. The Navy SEALs specialize in quick and direct action strike operations on naval targets but also train and work with US allies. During war, SEALs are often the specialized forces who take control of a target such as a ship, dam, or bridge. They also go door-to-door searching for enemies.

down, then beat you down some more," he wrote in *American Sniper*.[3] Kyle was nervous. But he was also ready to take on the ultimate challenge.

Cold, Wet, and Miserable

At 6 feet 2 inches (2 m) and 220 pounds (100 kg), Kyle was in good shape.[4] But no amount of swimming laps and weightlifting had prepared him for BUD/S. He sailed through the indoctrination period when contests of will and strength were tough but not impossible. But he was shocked to realize just how difficult phase one, physical conditioning, turned out to be. All recruits were required to do at least 100 sit-ups and 100 push-ups in two minutes and 20 pull-ups at a minimum. They were forced to swim in the ice-cold ocean for 500 yards (457 m), wearing

SURVIVAL TRAINING 101

When engaged in war, Navy SEALs face many dangerous obstacles—including the possibility of capture. It is therefore important that recruits are taught how to survive under pressure in a wide variety of situations. To prepare, all Navy SEALs must enroll in the Survival, Escape, Resistance, and Evasion (SERE) course. Often taught by former US prisoners of war (POWs), the SERE classes teach trainees basic and advanced survival techniques such as how to survive on the land, evade capture by enemy forces, resist interrogation, and escape from a camp should enemy capture occur.

A group of Navy SEAL recruits prepares for a swim in San Diego Bay.

heavy fins, in fewer than nine minutes. And they had to complete at least a 1.5-mile (2.4 km) run on the sand, dressed in boots and pants.[5] It felt similar to running a marathon without any preparation—three times per week before sunrise.

Then there was Hell Week. For nearly six days of around-the-clock training and tests on what they had learned, Kyle and the other SEAL recruits were subjected to 132 hours of rigorous, punishing exercise. Running, swimming, jumping, slogging through wet sand, carrying heavy metal boats on their heads—while instructors screamed orders and hosed them with freezing water. Flashbang (nonlethal) grenades exploded in the background for extra effect.

In one particularly grueling activity, Kyle and his team were taken out in a boat for seven nautical miles (13 km), dumped into the frigid water, and told to swim back to shore. "Getting through BUD/S and being a SEAL [was] more about mental toughness than anything else," Kyle wrote in his memoir. "Being stubborn and refusing to give in [was] the key to success."[6]

According to the Navy SEAL website, on average, 25 percent of recruits make it through Hell Week.[7] The rest are told to consider other military paths. For those more than five days of torture, Kyle was pummeled, verbally abused, and ready to pass out at any second. But he crossed the finish line. Barely.

COFFEE AND A DOUGHNUT

Most Navy SEAL recruits will admit that because of sleep deprivation and backbreaking exercise regimens, Hell Week lives up to its name. But for those who cannot make it, there is another option. If recruits ring a brass bell in the corner of the testing area during training, they are taken outside and treated to warm coffee and a doughnut. Yes, their pain is over. But the penalty is being kicked out of BUD/S immediately.

An Accidental Setback

In the second phase of BUD/S, recruits are taught combat swimming techniques, as well as scuba and

THE FIRST FROGMEN

SEALs see a lot of action in today's combat missions overseas. But these multifaceted navy sailors, sometimes called "frogmen," actually got their start during World War II (1939–1945). Part of small groups known as Underwater Demolition Teams (UDT), these warriors were called on to place explosives underneath enemy submarines without being noticed. Since that time, the SEALs have played a role in virtually every war the United States has been involved in, from the Korean War (1950–1953) to the Vietnam War (1954–1975), and the ongoing Iraq War. With time, the SEALs have also expanded their reach. These days, navy frogmen have taken to the sky and land, conquering cold climates and covering dusty desert terrain.

long-distance diving. Similar to phase one, they are tested on prior material. When Kyle began his diving training, he quickly discovered it was not a skill he had mastered. He was slower than the other guys. And he could not get the hang of being in the water for extended periods. Before long, his lack of sea legs caught up with him.

To do a deep dive successfully, it is important to keep the pressure in the inner and outer ears equalized. Most divers do this by popping the pressure out—pinching their nose while blowing out air at the same time. This relieves the pressure. During one of Kyle's initial dives, he failed to pop his ears correctly. The built-up pressure perforated his

Part of BUD/S training involves underwater exercises and learning how to safely use scuba gear.

eardrum, causing blood to pour out of his ears, eyes, and nose when he swam back to the surface.

Despite this gruesome scene, Kyle's injuries were not that serious. Still, after a trip to the doctor, he was ordered to take a leave of absence so he could recover. Luckily he was not dropped from the BUD/S program altogether. He would need to wait until the next class of SEAL recruits came through before continuing his studies.

Success at Last

By the time Kyle finished the second and third phases of BUD/S, he was more physically worn out and mentally drained than he had ever been in his life. But he had also accomplished a seemingly impossible goal. He had successfully made it through BUD/S. Along with 24 other men—less than 10 percent of his class—he was that much closer to becoming a Navy SEAL.

Kyle had to jump over a few more hurdles. He would have to master his fear of heights and go through three weeks of basic parachute training. Then he would endure eight more weeks of SEAL qualification training, learning mission planning, battle techniques, and SEAL-specific regulations and procedures. Finally, he would be required to dress in full uniform for a formal BUD/S class graduation ceremony. Then, and only then, could he officially wear the trident, the prized golden metal badge that distinguished him as a fully qualified Navy SEAL.

"I wanted to defend my country, do my duty, and do my job. I wanted, more than anything, to experience the thrill of battle."[8]
—Chris Kyle, in his autobiography

The badge features an eagle holding a US
Navy anchor, trident, and a pistol.

As 2001 began, Kyle was on the verge of realizing
his dreams. In no time at all, he would be shipped off to
combat, and everything he learned in BUD/S would be
put to the test. He had been assigned to SEAL Team 3,
a team that had already seen action in the Middle East
and would likely return. "I wanted to get into the heat if
I could. I think all of us did," Kyle wrote in his memoir.[9]
What's more, he would soon stumble across something
else that could inspire him to be the best man he could
possibly be: love.

CHAPTER
FOUR

A CHANCE ENCOUNTER

One evening in April 2001, a few weeks after BUD/S graduation, Chris decided to go to Maloney's Tavern in San Diego, California. Every so often he and his Navy SEAL buddies would get together to shoot some pool, have a couple of drinks, and try to pick up women. This night was no different—or so he thought.

Looking around the bar, Chris spotted a gorgeous woman. "My first impression was that she was beautiful, even if she looked [annoyed] about something," Chris wrote in his memoir. "When we started talking, I also found out she was smart, and had a good sense of humor. I sensed right away she was someone who could keep up with me."[1]

The woman Chris had approached was named Taya Studebaker—and he was right. She had not wanted to come to the bar that evening. She lived in Long Beach,

---

Taya Studebaker was not looking to find her future husband the night she joined a friend at Maloney's Tavern.

California, two hours away by car—a drive that was too long. Plus she was in a grumpy mood. Since moving to Long Beach a few months prior, she had not made many friends. She hated her job as a pharmaceutical saleswoman. And her luck at dating was terrible. Taya's friend had dragged her along to Maloney's Tavern in hopes of cheering her up and getting her mind off her worries.

Different Impressions

As soon as they began talking, Chris was sure he had met the woman of his dreams. He had dated a few women in the past, but none of them seemed on par with Taya. He asked her all sorts of questions. Then she asked Chris a few of her own. When she brought up what he did for a living, Chris told Taya he drove an ice cream truck. He was not sure what she believed about the military and did not want her to make any snap judgments.

But Taya was not fooled; she saw right through Chris's game. Her sister's ex-husband had also trained as a Navy SEAL, and Taya could see the signs from a mile away. "I know all about you guys. . . . You're arrogant, self-centered, and glory-seeking," Taya told Chris after he finally admitted his job as a SEAL. "You lie and you think you can do whatever you want."[2]

Taya insisted she did not want to date a Navy SEAL, let alone marry one. But Chris would not give up. He asked for her phone number and was elated when she eventually gave it to him.

Wedding Bells

After that night at the bar, Chris and Taya's relationship was slow to start. He called her the next morning. And the day after that. And for weeks after that. Even though she was always delighted to talk to him, Taya never called him on her own nor made the first move. For the first few months of their courtship, Chris was the one laying on all the romance.

"SEALs almost never admit to strangers what they really do, and Chris had some of the best . . . stories ever. One of the better ones was dolphin waxer: he claimed that dolphins in captivity need to be waxed so their skin didn't disintegrate. . . . He's also convinced girls that he mans an ATM machine sitting inside and doling out money when people put their cards in."[3]

—Taya Kyle

Then something in their relationship shifted. Little by little, Taya began to trust Chris—particularly after the events in New York City on September 11, 2001. After they watched the coverage on television of two

The attacks on September 11, 2001, caused
shock and anger among Americans.

planes flying into the World Trade Center buildings, Taya felt closer to Chris than she had ever before. "We are, in many ways, opposites. Still, we seemed to click. . . . He seemed to pick up on how I was feeling, sometimes before I did. And he let me express that emotion, and, importantly, gave me space."[4]

By the time one year had passed since that fateful meeting at Maloney's Tavern, Chris and Taya were already talking about marriage. In February 2002, the Navy SEAL Team 3 received word that they would be deployed to Kuwait in the Middle East in a few weeks. The couple wanted to get married before Chris departed. "The decision stunned me, even as I made it,"

SEPTEMBER 11, 2001

On Tuesday, September 11, 2001, one of the most horrific events in history took place on US soil. Nineteen al-Qaeda terrorists from Saudi Arabia, the United Arab Emirates, Lebanon, and Egypt hijacked four commercial airplanes with men, women, and children on board. One plane flew into the Pentagon in Arlington, Virginia. At 8:46 a.m., Flight 11 struck floors 93 to 99 in the North Tower of the World Trade Center in New York City. At 9:03 a.m., Flight 175 crashed into floors 77 to 85 in the World Trade Center's South Tower. Between 16,400 and 18,000 people were inside the buildings when the attack occurred. Most made it to safety before both buildings collapsed. When the passengers on the fourth plane, Flight 93, heard about the attacks, they fought back against the terrorists and managed to divert the plane into an empty field in Western Pennsylvania. All told, nearly 3,000 people died—2,753 in New York, 184 at the Pentagon, and 40 on Flight 93.[5]

Chris said. "I agreed with it. It was completely logical. We were definitely in love. I knew she was the woman I wanted to spend my life with."[6]

Chris and Taya got married in the mountains of Nevada on March 16, 2002. It was a small affair, with Taya's friends and family from Oregon and Chris's SEAL friends and relatives from Texas. In her wedding vows, Taya told Chris, "I will remind you who you are when you forget." Chris inscribed Taya's wedding ring with the words, "All of me. My love, my life."[7]

Separation

Not long after the ceremony, it was time for Chris to return to his duties. Though Taya wanted more time to spend with her new husband, she also knew how much he valued his work.

Chris and Taya were excited for marriage even though they knew
it would be a difficult road ahead with Chris's deployment.

Meanwhile, a global catastrophe was about to explode. Since the attacks on September 11, emotions had been running high all across the United States and around the world. Who was responsible for such violent acts of terrorism? Was it President Saddam Hussein's corrupt government in Iraq? Did it have to do with oil and money? Hatred from religious extremists? Or a combination of all three? The American people wanted answers, and it was up to their government and the military to figure out a way to deliver them.

In September 2002, Chris shipped out to Kuwait and the Persian Gulf, off the coast of Iraq. He and the rest of SEAL Team 3 would spend the next few months on Visit, Board, Search, and Seize (VBSS) duty. Billions of dollars in excess oil and other valuable items— potentially weapons of mass destruction—were being smuggled illegally out of Iraq on huge cargo ships. It was the US government's hope that the Navy SEALs could put a stop to the practice.

Taya was worried about her husband's deployment. But though Chris loved his wife, after three years of preparation he was ready to head overseas and do the job he trained for. He hoped he and his fellow SEALs would finally see some action. Little did he know, his wish would soon be granted.

PRECIOUS CARGO

In 2002 to 2003, prior to the start of the Iraq War, the United States was keeping a close watch on tankers in the Persian Gulf. It was rumored that Iraq was smuggling all sorts of materials to and from countries such as Syria, Iran, and Turkey, in exchange for money used to fund potential terrorist efforts throughout the Middle East and around the world. The biggest commodity was oil. The United Nations (UN) established the Oil-for-Food Programme to enable Iraq to sell its oil in exchange for food, medicine, and other necessary supplies. Hussein secretly took a portion of the oil to sell illegally. Because of the trade embargos and economic restrictions the UN had placed on Iraq following the Persian Gulf War (1990–1991), Iraq was smuggling other items in addition to oil. Cigarettes were a popular item, as were weapons.

CHAPTER
FIVE

THE UNITED STATES GOES TO WAR

B y 2003, the US government had lost its patience with Hussein and had asked him to resign. The United States suspected Hussein's corrupt regime was developing weapons of mass destruction, hiding and supporting terrorists, and committing human rights abuses against the Iraqi people, and the practices needed to stop. Since 2001, US President George W. Bush had been lobbying the US Congress to authorize use of military force in Iraq with the hope of forcibly ousting Hussein. In March 2003, the United Nations (UN) and Congress voted for action.

On the morning of March 20, 2003, Kyle and the rest of SEAL Team 3—called Charlie Platoon—piled into a series of air force helicopters headed from Kuwait to Iraq. They, along with thousands of marines and British allied troops, were part of the platoons tasked with taking control of coastal oil refineries before the

US Navy battle helicopters touch down in Iraq in March 2003.

> "American and coalition forces are in the early stages of military operations to disarm Iraq, to free its people and to defend the world from grave danger. . . . We come to Iraq with respect for its citizens, for their great civilization and for the religious faiths they practice. We have no ambition in Iraq, except to remove a threat and restore control of that country to its own people. . . . We will pass through this time of peril and carry on the work of peace. We will defend our freedom. We will bring freedom to others. And we will prevail."[3]
> —President George W. Bush authorizing military action in Iraq

Iraqis could have the buildings destroyed. The Iraqis had burned thousands of oil wells and contaminated much of their surrounding areas during the earlier Persian Gulf War, and the US government wanted to prevent the same thing from happening again.

Meanwhile, US warships stationed in the Persian Gulf fired missiles into the air while US warplanes dropped 2,000-pound (910 kg) bombs on military targets elsewhere in Iraq.[1] It was a full-scale attack. The Iraq War had begun.

Inside the helicopters, the SEALs were packed into desert patrol vehicles (DPVs)—jeep-like vehicles designed for driving in the desert. They were wearing gas masks and full protective gear in case of a chemical attack on the ground. Kyle and the rest of Charlie Platoon were pumped and ready to go. "My war was finally here," Kyle said.[2]

Kyle was ready to put all of his training and hard work
to the test when he was called to serve overseas.

A Rough Start

As soon as the helicopters hit the ground outside the al-Faw oil refinery, their rear doors popped open. Bullets from the Iraqi forces stationed outside the refinery's gate flew everywhere and grenades exploded left and right. The DPVs sped down the ramps at top speeds but, suddenly, stopped. Instead of dry sand on the ground, there was oil-soaked dirt. The wheels of the jeeps were stuck in the sludge. Kyle and the SEALs were not deterred by the setback. They disembarked and continued toward the perimeter of the refinery on foot as smoke and dust clouded the scene. "You'd hear the rounds coming past you in the air—*errrrrrrrrr*—then you'd here the echo—*erhrhrrhrh*, followed closely by secondary explosions and whatever other havocs the bullets caused," Kyle wrote in his memoir. "This is great. I . . . love this. It's nerve-wracking and exciting and I . . . love it."[4]

The battle continued on into the night. When British troops arrived the next morning, what was left of the Iraqi forces had already retreated from the scene. The fight to secure the al-Faw oil refinery was only one of many more to come elsewhere in Iraq. It was time for

Kyle, the SEALs, and the rest of the US military to head toward Baghdad, the Iraqi capital, and oust Hussein from power.

A Difficult Choice

After a brief rotation back to Kuwait to replenish supplies, Charlie Platoon landed back in Iraq on the outskirts of an-Nasiriyah. This large city on the banks of the Euphrates River was a little more than three hours southeast from Baghdad by car. Charlie Platoon was there to assist the US Marines and Army Corps in taking over an-Nasiriyah and neutralizing "Ambush Alley"—a particularly dangerous area known for potential attacks

JESSICA LYNCH CAPTURED!

Kyle made it through the Battle of an-Nasiriyah safely. But some of the marines and army soldiers he was fighting alongside were not so lucky. Private First Class Jessica Lynch was also part of the 2003 invasion of Iraq. On March 23, her convoy drove off course and was ambushed. She was injured when her Humvee crashed, and then Iraqi forces captured her. For one week, Lynch was held captive at Saddam Hospital in an-Nasiriyah. Then, in a flurry of activity, US Special Operations Forces rescued her on April 1—she was the first US POW rescued since World War II and it was the first time a woman had ever been extracted. Although the media initially reported that she heroically fought off her aggressors, Lynch insisted her rifle had jammed and she had done nothing of the sort. "It does [bother me] that [the military] used me as a way to symbolize all this [war]," Lynch said to reporters. "It's wrong."[5]

Kyle worked hard to become a SEAL sniper.

by Iraqi forces. If the US military and their allies were successful, they would be able to cross the Saddam Canal, a waterway named for the Iraqi president, and secure a pathway to Baghdad.

Kyle was situated on the rooftop of a two-story building in a small town near an-Nasiriyah. The marines were coming through on foot, and it was Kyle's job to protect them by doing overwatch—keeping an eye out from above for any suspicious activity below. "I was still a new guy, a newbie or rookie in the Teams," Kyle wrote in his memoir. "I was also not yet trained as a SEAL sniper. I wanted to be one in the worst way, but I had a long way to go."[6]

Looking through the scope of his rifle, Kyle watched as a few marines got out of their jeeps and started searching the area. Suddenly, an Iraqi woman exited one of the buildings and pulled something out from under her clothes. It was a grenade. Kyle took aim and fired, killing her instantly. The grenade exploded, but none of the marines were hurt.

The woman on the ground was the first person Kyle had killed with a sniper rifle—and the only time he would ever kill anyone other than a man during his

IRAQI LEADERS

The US government had its reasons for authorizing military use in Iraq—oil, combatting terrorism, and fear. Though most Americans supported the troops, many seemed torn about whether the actual decision to invade was the "right" one. Regular citizens in Iraq were also divided on the issue. Many had grown resentful of Hussein's corrupt rule. Why did he and his family get to enjoy wealth and comfort whereas regular people were often without food, running water, and adequate electricity? Why were so many artists, thinkers, and hardworking Muslims thrown into prison for no reason? These Iraqis were thankful for the United States' help.

On the other hand, a deeper religious issue was at stake. Most of the world's Muslims are Sunni—Muslims who believe in a more orthodox, or traditional, interpretation of the Koran and that the leader of Islam should be appointed by election and consensus. In Iraq, the situation is reversed—there are more Shiites than Sunnis. Shiites believe descendants of Muhammad should lead Islam.

four tours of duty in Iraq. "It was my duty to shoot, and I don't regret it. The woman was already dead. I was just making sure she didn't take any marines with her," Kyle said.[7]

The Battle of an-Nasiriyah was one of the bloodiest during the first phase of the Iraq War. Many people, both Americans and Iraqis, died fighting for their cause. On April 1, 2003, the US and allied forces took control of an-Nasiriyah, paving the way for a direct route to Baghdad—and Hussein. A few weeks after Kyle made his first fatal shot, he and Charlie Platoon were rotated back to the United States.

Back Home

Being back in the United States was tough for Kyle. In *American Sniper*, he wrote Americans' lack of support for the war and the US military frustrated him. He also felt out of place among all the material comforts of home. He missed his buddies in Charlie Platoon and wanted to be back by their side. And he was angry his platoon was removed from the fighting so quickly.

Kyle also had to deal with psychological side effects. According to his wife, Kyle had trouble sleeping and barely left the house. Loud noises such as car horns or sudden movements bothered him. And talking about his experiences in Iraq was out of the question.

But Kyle did have two things to be thankful for while he was home on leave. For one, he enrolled in both sniper school and navigator school. There, he learned not only how to properly aim and shoot a sniper rifle, but also how to camouflage his uniform and sneak into position without being seen. He also became a father to his son, Colton.

SHARK!

One of the most shocking moments Kyle experienced during training was after sniper school had concluded. He was tasked to swim across the San Diego Bay to plant a mine underneath a ship. Along the journey he felt a sharp pull on one of the swim fins attached to his feet. It was a shark! Luckily he got away by cutting the rubber shoe off using a knife he kept in his swim gear. Shortly thereafter, he was rescued by a security boat and brought to safety.

Only ten days after his son was born—nearly one year after he left Iraq the first time, Kyle received orders that he was needed back in Iraq. "I felt bad about leaving Taya. She was still healing from the birth," he wrote in his memoir. "But at the same time, I felt my duty as a SEAL was more important. I wanted to get back into action. I wanted to go to war."[8]

CHAPTER
SIX

TOURS OF DUTY

A lot had changed in Iraq as a result of the war since Kyle left in the spring of 2003. Baghdad was liberated on April 9, 2003. Iraqi leader Hussein was captured eight months later in December and removed from office. But despite the US-backed, Iraq-run interim government that had been put into place, terrorist forces were still on the rise. Some were jihadists, Islamic fundamentalists who believed in carrying out acts of aggression against nonbelievers. Others were members of al-Qaeda, radical Sunni Muslims led by Osama bin Laden. There was still a lot to do before Iraq would be stable enough to govern on its own.

For the next six years, Kyle would return to Iraq three times as a sniper, first with SEAL Team 3, and then with a sister platoon, Delta Platoon. In 2004, he participated in the siege to regain control of Fallujah, a city southwest of Baghdad, from insurgents. In 2006, he took part in the fight for Ramadi, a city in the western part of Iraq. And in 2008, he returned one last time for

Kyle's strong sense of duty to his country carried him through his four tours in the Middle East.

combat in Sadr City, one of the most dangerous sections of Baghdad that was full of insurgents.

During each tour, as with all military personnel, Kyle risked his life for his fellow SEALs and members of the US military. He pulled off some of the most record-setting sniper shots in US history. And he would lose the two soldiers he was closest to during his duty. But Kyle was committed to becoming the best sharpshooter in the United States. "I thought about the casualties I'd seen, and the fact that I could be the next one carried out. But I wasn't going to quit," he wrote in his memoir.[1]

Fallujah

On November 7, 2004, members of SEAL Teams 3, 5, and 8 joined between 10,000 and 15,000 US soldiers and marines in their entrance into Fallujah, a city in Iraq's

SADDAM HUSSEIN CAPTURED

"Ladies and gentlemen, we got him," US administrator Paul Bremer announced to a swarm of journalists in Baghdad.[2] On December 13, 2003, US troops stormed a small farmhouse located on the outskirts of Tikrit, Iraq. Inside, down a 6- to 8-foot (1.8 to 2.5 m) hole beneath a cellar floor covered up by a rug, former Iraqi leader Hussein was hiding. He had a gun and more than $750,000 in cash.[3] When soldiers discovered him, the 66-year-old disheveled Hussein, sporting a long gray and white beard, surrendered without any struggle.

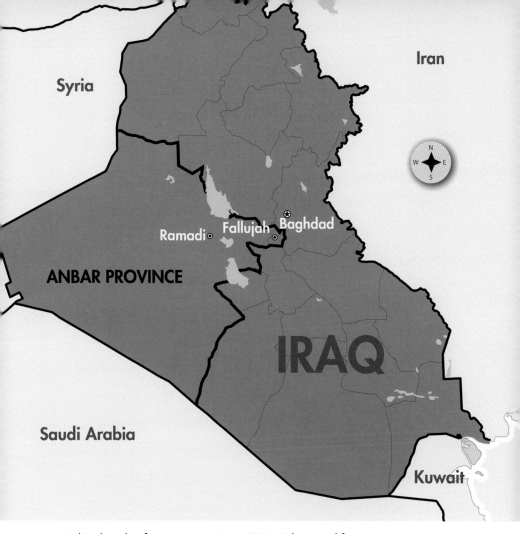

In his decade of service as a Navy SEAL, Kyle served four tours of duty throughout Iraq—in Fallujah, Ramadi, and Baghdad.

Anbar Province.[4] They were tasked with helping Iraqis loyal to the interim government regain control from nearly 4,000 rebel insurgents. A city of narrow streets, mosque domes, and sparse vegetation, Fallujah was riddled with flying bullets, swirling dust clouds, and deafening explosions.

Clad in his signature hiking boots and baseball cap, 30-year-old Kyle and the rest of his crew evacuated more than 250 civilians from an apartment complex on the northwest edge of Fallujah and set up position. He used a baby crib to prop up his sniper rifle and waited for action. "Looking out the window, I was anxious for the battle to start," Kyle said. "I wanted a target . . . [and] I didn't have to wait all that long."[5]

Block-by-block combat between Iraqi insurgents and US forces, primarily marines, raged for six weeks. Kyle was injured when a rocket-propelled grenade hit the building he was in, sending a pile of rubble crumbling down onto his legs and pinning him to the wall. It took nearly three weeks for his bruised and bloodied legs to heal. But by Thanksgiving, he was back on the job. He even took a short break from the fighting with his buddies to eat a Thanksgiving meal of turkey, mashed potatoes, and stuffing on a rooftop.

The Battle of Fallujah turned out to be the bloodiest in the Iraq War and some of the nastiest fighting US Marines had witnessed since the Vietnam War. Approximately 100 US troops died. Six hundred more were wounded.[6]

Elections were held on January 30, 2005, and a new Shia-dominant, Iraq-run transitional government was ushered into power. Grand Ayatollah Ali al-Sistani of the United Iraqi Alliance became the new leader. And Kyle was ready for a quick recharge.

Kyle did return to California in the spring of 2005. But after being home for nine months, he was already bored, alienated, and ready to be a sniper once again. "I was trained for war. I was made for it. My country was at war and it needed me," he wrote in his memoir. "And I missed it. I missed the excitement and the thrill."[7]

2005 IRAQI ELECTIONS

On January 30, 2005, nearly two years after the overthrow of Hussein, tens of thousands of Iraqis turned out to vote in the first free election in their country in 50 years. Voters could choose between 111 parties for members of regional parliaments and elect a 275-member national assembly that would write the Iraqi constitution the following October. According to news outlets such as the New York Times, 60 percent of Iraqis cast their ballots despite widespread threats and risk of suicide bombers.[8] "We feel now that we are human beings living in this country," a 25-year-old man named Muhammad Abdul-Ridha, told a reporter. "Now I feel I have a responsibility, I have a vote. Things will go right if people leave us alone to do what we want to do. If they leave the Iraqi people to decide for themselves, things will get better."[9] In December 2005, more elections were held—this time for a parliament that would serve a four-year term. Nearly 11 million Iraqis turned out to vote.[10] This was considered a true victory for democracy.

The Devil of Ramadi

While he was home, Kyle become a father for a second time—this time, to a baby girl named McKenna. But still, he reenlisted against his wife's wishes. In April 2006, only two days after his daughter was born, he deployed to Ramadi, a city 30 miles (50 km) west of Fallujah.

Kyle's five months in Ramadi were groundbreaking for many reasons. For one, he developed a reputation among the insurgents. The US Marines already referred to him as the Legend because of his knack for escaping death. Now, because he was close to setting a record for most sniper kills by a US soldier, the Iraqis started calling him *al-Shaitan Ramadi*, "the Devil of Ramadi." They also put an $80,000 bounty on his head. "It made me feel proud," Kyle said when he heard the news. "The fact is, I was just one guy, and they had singled me out for causing them a lot of damage. They wanted me gone. I had to feel good about that."[11]

But Kyle's experience in Ramadi was not all ego boosting and glory filled. It was there that he endured his first major psychological setback. During a particularly volatile engagement with Iraqi rebels on

Kyle was a target for Iraqi insurgents since he
had killed many of their top men.

Kyle and his fellow SEALs were assigned dangerous missions that could result in deadly injuries.

August 2, fellow SEAL Ryan Job was hit in the face with a bullet and permanently blinded. At the time, Kyle and 25-year-old Job were stationed as a two-man sniper team on overwatch duty—Kyle on the gun and Job as his observer. When the attack occurred, Job was the one who got hit with the bullet.

Hours later, another close friend, 28-year-old Marc Lee, was shot through the mouth during a building raid. Lee later died from his wounds. He was the first SEAL casualty since the Iraq War began three years earlier.

More Bad News

After Lee's death, Kyle and the rest of his unit were temporarily unavailable for service so they could rest and mourn. Though Job survived his injuries, Kyle believed he was responsible for not preventing them from happening to Job. He fell into a deep depression.

When the call came from Taya one month later that their daughter might have leukemia, which ended up being a false alarm, Kyle knew he had to go home. The impact of Lee's death and Job's injuries had taken a toll on his mental health. Kyle continued to feel torn about abandoning his other family—the SEALs. "It was a conflict—family and country, family and brothers in arms—that I never really resolved," he said. "I still felt like a quitter, a guy who didn't do enough."[12]

RYAN JOB

Ryan Job was born in 1981 in a small town near Seattle, Washington. On August 2, 2006, while he was serving as a Navy SEAL, he was hit by a sniper bullet in Ramadi, Iraq, and blinded in both eyes. For the next three years, Job would undergo many surgeries to help restore his vision. Despite his impairment, he climbed Mount Hood in Oregon and Mount Rainer in Washington. He also participated in a triathlon and married his longtime girlfriend in 2007. Two years later, the couple was expecting their first child. Job died suddenly on September 24, 2009, during recovery from reconstructive surgery on his eyes. His wife, Kelly, and their daughter, Leah, survive him.

CHAPTER
SEVEN

RETURN TO CIVILIAN LIFE

B y 2009, Chris, now 35, was facing a decision. He had just concluded another tour in Sadr City, Iraq—the most dangerous area in Baghdad. It was there that he shot his longest kill from 2,100 yards (1,920 m) away—the length of 21 football fields. Plus he set the record for most confirmed kills by a US sniper at 160 officially documented shots.[1] Would he reenlist when this tour of duty was over?

For Chris, there was no question he was at the prime of his military career. But aside from the mounting stress of war, his excessively high blood pressure, and post-traumatic stress disorder (PTSD), Chris was facing a different battle at home. Ever since their son, Colton, was born, Taya had become fed up with her husband's behavior. She knew how important the SEALs were to him, but his die-hard attention toward his job had come at the expense of his marriage and relationship with

Chris and Taya had to work hard to get their marriage back on track after he returned home from war.

his kids. So she gave him an ultimatum: your job or your family:

> I've always believed that your responsibility is to God, family, and country—in that order. [Chris] disagreed—he put country ahead of family. . . . He always said, 'if you tell me not to reenlist, I won't.' But I couldn't do that. I told him, 'I can't tell you what to do. You'll just hate me and resent me all your life. . . . If you do reenlist, then I will know exactly where we stand. It will change things. I won't want it to, but I know in my heart it will.'[2]

In the end, despite intense feelings of guilt for leaving the SEALs, Chris chose his family.

Marital Problems

Chris did not want a divorce. But when he arrived home in San Diego after Sadr City, he harbored a lot of resentment, particularly toward Taya. "I felt like she knew who I was when she met me. She knew I was a warrior. That was all I'd ever wanted to do," he said.[3] Plus "after years of being in war zones and separated from my wife, I think in a way I'd just forgotten what it means to be in love—the responsibilities that come with it, like truly listening and sharing."[4]

So rather than try to make up for lost time, Chris pushed Taya away. He started texting old girlfriends and

Despite her reservations about Chris's time overseas, Taya wanted
to be a supportive wife and allow Chris to do what he loved.

TATTOOS

There were many reasons for Taya and Chris's marital spats. Taya also had issues with her husband's tattoos. In a word, she hated them. On the inside of one of his arms, he got a trident to represent his love and respect for the Navy SEALs. On the front he inked a crusader cross because he wanted everyone to know he was a Christian. The cross was red for blood.

ignored his kids. He spent many nights out drinking with his buddies. He even got arrested for acting rowdy and starting bar fights. Taya talked him into going to marriage counseling, but the sessions did not seem to help their marriage.

It soon became clear to Chris that his family was not enough to keep his brain occupied. What he desperately needed was a purpose now that his sniper career was over. So he began searching for ways to fill up his days that would enable him to put the skills he developed as a Navy SEAL to good use. He dreamed of starting a military training facility for US servicemen, wealthy businessmen, and cops, but he was short on cash. In late 2009, however, he met someone who could help make his vision a reality—a rich hedge-fund manager named J. Kyle Bass.

For months Bass had been searching for a former Navy SEAL who could be a bodyguard. He was also

When Kyle arrived home after his tours, he kept up with some of his favorite hobbies, including hunting.

hoping to hire a security consultant on a house he was building in Texas. Chris was perfect for the job.

Before long, Bass and Chris were drawing up the paperwork for Chris's new business. It would be called Craft International (CI), with training sites in Arizona and Texas. Craft International's logo would be a skull representing Chris's life and military service. During Thanksgiving and Christmas, Chris and his family relocated back to Midlothian so he could run operations from CI's corporate offices in Dallas.

Giving Back

Kyle's new job was rewarding. But he still spent most of his off time drinking and carousing in bars. One night, he had too much to drink and drove off the road, crashing his truck to pieces. He nearly died. The thought of leaving his kids without a father scared him. It was time for Kyle to stop feeling miserable and to get his life back on track.

"The accident woke me up. I'm sorry to say that I needed something like that to get my head back straight," he said. "I think I [now] realize everything I have, and everything I could lose. And I also understand not just where my responsibilities are but how to fulfill them."[5]

As with everything else Kyle had done in his life, he invested all of his energy in getting better. He went to church more often. He started eating healthier food, drank less alcohol, and made more of an effort to exercise and get a good night's sleep. At his wife's suggestion, they went back to marriage counseling

"The story behind the Craft skull logo combines several meaningful pieces of Chris Kyle's life and service to this great nation but mainly honors his fallen teammates. As part of SEAL Team 3, Chris and his fellow teammates painted similar skulls on their gear in order to strike fear in the enemy. The crosshair symbolizes his time spent on a sniper rifle and is also in the form of a Templar cross to symbolize his faith. Lastly, the crosshair is on the right eye to honor SO2 Ryan Job USN (SEAL), who was critically wounded when he was shot in the right eye while on deployment to Iraq in 2006."[6]
—Craft International

In order to help himself heal from PTSD, Kyle reached out to other veterans and worked with them by talking or by taking them to nearby gun ranges.

and planned more romantic evenings together. And he started spending more time with his kids—taking his daughter to dance class, coaching his son's T-ball team, and taking the entire family to a Six Flags amusement park.

Outside the home, Kyle focused on giving back as well. He volunteered his time for Lone Survivor Foundation and Troops First, groups working toward physically and mentally rehabilitating wounded soldiers through educational courses and healing retreats. And in 2011, he started an organization of his own, the FITCO Cares Foundation, a nonprofit organization dedicated to donating in-home fitness equipment to war veterans as part of their Heroes Project:

What wounded veterans don't need is sympathy. They need to be treated like the men they are: equals, heroes, and people who still have tremendous value for society. . . . I'm not suggesting we give vets handouts; what people need are hand-ups—a little opportunity and strategic help.[7]

"The opportunity to exercise is such an important part of a healthy, well balanced life but it can sometimes be intimidating to walk in to a gym if veterans feel like they don't quite measure up to everyone else there. . . . Imagine how self-conscious you might feel as a wounded veteran, walking in to a gym with a prosthetic limb, with significant burns over a portion of your body, or [with] the anxiety of being around large groups of people brought on by Post Traumatic Stress Disorder. These are the people the FITCO Cares 'Heroes Project' was created to serve."[8]

—*FITCO Cares President Travis Cox*

Becoming an Author

Perhaps one of the biggest achievements Kyle accomplished in the years following his sniper career was becoming a published author. At first, when an editor from HarperCollins approached him with the idea

of writing a book about his life, Kyle was skeptical.
He did not want it to seem like he was bragging when
some of his friends had died during the war. Plus he had
never written a book before, let alone one that involved
the military.

But when Jim DeFelice, an author with more
than 50 books to his name, agreed to cowrite the
autobiography, and attorney Scott McEwen came on
board to fact-check and consult, Chris finally gave
in. It also helped that Taya would be contributing by

FROM A COAUTHOR'S PERSPECTIVE

When DeFelice was approached about coauthoring *American Sniper*, he said he would need to talk to Kyle first before making a decision. According to DeFelice, it did not take much convincing. "I'd say that within five minutes of the [initial] call with Chris, I was onboard," DeFelice said. "The way he talked about his dead friends and the fact that he wanted to give their families the money from the book convinced me that I had to be involved."[9] From that point forward, the writing process went smoothly.

Kyle shared his stories about the Iraq War while DeFelice took notes. DeFelice interviewed Kyle's friends, colleagues, and family members to corroborate Kyle's stories. During their off time, the two men played video games. When the book was published, DeFelice was pleased with the result. "The story had to tell what a warrior *really* was thinking. . . . I wanted to show people exactly how you have to narrow the world down to black and white when you are at war," he said.[10]

STARS EARN STRIPES

In addition to becoming a published author in 2012, Kyle did something he never thought he would do: appear on reality television. In *Stars Earn Stripes*, a competitive show in which celebrities participated in real military missions and exercises, Kyle and teammate Dean Cain drove through land mines, soared through green smoke in a helicopter, and fired short-range missiles at targets. Kyle enjoyed his experience on the show and had a lot of fun working with Cain. The NBC show was taken off the air because of its questionable glorification of war and violence.

writing some passages from her perspective. Chris also had DeFelice agree that he would be free to write the book as he saw fit—no politically correct terminology or censorship allowed. Chris wanted to be able to describe Iraqi insurgents as "savages" throughout the book.

When *American Sniper: The Autobiography of the Most Lethal Sniper in U.S. Military History* was published on January 3, 2012, Kyle was thrilled about the accomplishment. In fact, he enjoyed putting his thoughts down on paper so much that he began researching what would later become *American Gun: A History of the U.S. in Ten Firearms*.

In February 2013, at the time of his death, Kyle was more settled than he had ever been since leaving the SEALs in 2009. He loved being a faithful husband and devoted father to his kids. He was doing what he could

Kyle worked with actor Dean Cain on the television show *Stars Earn Stripes*.

to help wounded veterans heal. And he felt more at peace about not being in active combat. In a sense, Kyle had served his country well abroad. Now he was doing so at home.

"Being a SEAL has been a huge part of me. I still feel the pull. I certainly would have preferred having the best of both worlds—the job *and* the family," he wrote at the end of his memoir. "I'm not the same guy I was when I first went to war. No one is. Before you're in combat, you have this innocence about you. Then, all of a sudden, you see this whole other side of life. I don't regret any of it. I'd do it again."[11]

CHAPTER
EIGHT

MURDERED IN COLD BLOOD

Despite his work helping struggling veterans, Kyle's life would end in tragedy. After the assassination of Kyle and Littlefield at Rough Creek Lodge on February 2, 2013, people around the world were shocked by the news that a bullet had ended the life of the United States' top sniper. The only person who was not surprised was the man who had pulled the trigger—Eddie Ray Routh. In fact, he was elated.

Barely one hour after Routh murdered Kyle and Littlefield in cold blood, he appeared at the door of his sister Laura's house with a new set of keys in his hand. He announced he was the proud owner of a new vehicle. "I sold my soul for a truck. We went up to the gun range. I killed them," Routh said. "Chris and his friend. I killed them. I murdered them."[1]

When Laura looked out and saw the fancy black truck in her driveway, she knew her long-troubled

Photos of Routh posing with machine guns and other rifles during his time in the military were used in his trial in February 2015.

brother was telling the truth. She begged him to turn himself in. Routh gave Laura a hug, told her he loved her, and left. She immediately called the police and explained what had happened.

Later that evening, the cops caught up to Routh at his parents' house in Lancaster, Texas, where he was living at the time. They questioned him for approximately 15 minutes, but Routh left the house before they could find out anything substantial. Racing after him with

POST-TRAUMATIC STRESS DISORDER

In the four years leading up to the day he killed Kyle and Littlefield, Routh had exhibited the telltale signs of PTSD. He heard voices. He drank excessively. And he was prone to paranoid and violent outbursts, sometimes threatening his family with a knife or loaded gun. To fix the problem, doctors proscribed Routh an antidepressant called Zoloft; lithium, a prescription drug that treats mania; and prazosin, a drug that helps lessen nightmares. But according to Routh's parents, none of it helped. They then tried to commit Routh to psychiatric facilities. "He can't even carry on a conversation. I really think he needs to be in the hospital," Jodi begged a doctor.[2] But Routh was released every time.

PTSD is a powerful disease. According to the US Department of Veteran Affairs, nearly 8 percent of Americans will suffer from PTSD at some point in their lives—at least 20 percent of Iraqi war veterans are afflicted.[3] Experts are still trying to come up with new effective ways to treat the illness. It is important for family members of those dealing with PTSD to be patient in their search for a solution. Unfortunately for Routh, Kyle, and Littlefield, the cure did not come soon enough.

their lights flashing and sirens blaring, the cops engaged Routh in the type of high-speed car chase normally found on television. When they finally caught up to him near Dallas—18 miles (30 km) away—cuffed him, and drove him to the station, Routh confessed to everything. He was put in jail to await a trial.

Kyle's Funeral

Meanwhile on February 11, nine days after Routh's shooting spree, a public memorial service was held for Kyle. Close to 7,000 mourners filled AT&T Stadium in Dallas to pay their respects, including politicians such as former GOP vice presidential candidate Sarah Palin and celebrities such as Dallas Cowboys quarterback Troy Aikman.[4] Country music singer Randy Travis sang a moving tribute. Kyle's American flag–draped coffin sat at the 50-yard line.

Then a slideshow appeared on the Jumbotron, featuring pictures of Kyle taken in the course of his short life. Some photos were from his childhood and years as a rodeo star. Others were from his decade of service as a Navy SEAL and as a husband and father to Taya, Colton, and McKenna. Rod Stewart's song "Forever Young" and

AT&T Stadium was filled with members of the military who had come to pay their respects to Kyle and his family.

AC/DC's "Back in Black" played over the loudspeakers while the photographs flashed across the screen.

One by one, members of Kyle's Navy SEAL platoon gave eulogies in his honor. One read a letter from Kyle's parents, stating, "God anointed you with the name The Protector. Your life embodied the full meaning of that." As the service drew to a close, Taya walked up to the stage with tears in her eyes and quietly said a prayer for her departed husband. "Life has a way of working out," she said. "And you have showed me that in life, and even in death, some people are always with you. I love you, Chris. I love. I love you."[5]

The next morning, 200 motorcycles, police cars, and military vehicles escorted Kyle's body on its 200-mile (320 km) journey from Midlothian to the Texas State Cemetery in Austin, the capital of Texas. Flags were draped across bridges, and thousands of people lined the roads and highways to watch as a white hearse carried Kyle's coffin to his grave. One woman almost fainted as the car containing Taya drove by. "I just wanted to come out and support that amazing family," she said as she waved her US flag high in the air.[6]

A SHRINE

In military funerals, it is common for a fallen soldier's possessions to be displayed near his or her coffin. Kyle's funeral was no different. Called a "battle cross," Kyle's gun, boots, helmet, and jacket were configured in the shape of a cross and placed in the center of the stage during the memorial to commemorate his decade of honorable and noteworthy military service.

Routh's Trial

Exactly two years later, on February 11, 2015, Routh's trial began. Tim Moore, Routh's lawyer, argued for a verdict of not guilty by reason of insanity. "He thought in his mind, at that point in time, that it was either him or them, that he had to take their lives because, in his psychosis, he was thinking they were going to take his," Moore told the jury. "You will find that at the time of this tragic event, this tragic occurrence, that Eddie Routh was insane."[7]

There was no question Routh was guilty; he had confessed to killing Kyle and Littlefield without being coerced. But if Moore got his way and won the case, Routh would be released and committed to a mental hospital instead of receiving jail time.

What Taya and the prosecution wanted was a guilty verdict—for Routh to spend the rest of his life in prison without parole.

For the next few days, a series of witnesses took the stand. These included the first police officers to arrive at Rough Creek Lodge the day Kyle and Littlefield were murdered, Taya, and Routh's mother who insisted the doctors at Dallas veterans medical center were responsible for her son's deteriorated state. They had

> "Though we feel sadness and loss, know this: legends never die. Chris Kyle is not gone. Chris Kyle is everywhere. He is the fabric of the freedom that blessed the people of this great nation. He is forever embodied in the strength and tenacity of the SEAL teams, where his courageous path will be followed and his memory is enshrined as SEALs continue to ruthlessly hunt down and destroy America's enemies."[8]
> —from a speech given by a commander of Kyle's, at Kyle's funeral

Although Routh had confessed to killing Kyle and Littlefield, a trial still needed to be held.

given him too much medication, she argued, and failed to keep him locked up when he was a danger to himself and others.

By the end of two weeks, and after deliberating for less than two and a half hours, the jury—ten women and two men—reached a decision. On February 24, the judge read the verdict aloud to a rapt courtroom: Guilty. Life in prison without parole.

Despite the fact that capital punishment is still legal in Texas, Routh would not be put to death for what he had done. But he would spend the rest of his life behind

ROUTH'S TRIAL

During Routh's trial, a reporter from the *New Yorker* magazine traveled to a town near Amarillo, Texas, to pay Routh's parents a visit. When he asked the Rouths how they felt about the crime their son had committed, Jodi admitted they were devastated:

All I can think about in my mind is that, if they would have left him in the hospital, then those two men wouldn't be dead today. . . . My intention is that they step up and give these men . . . the treatment they deserve. . . . It's not just that they deserve it. They've already earned it. They've already served their time. They've already done what they were asked to do.[10]

bars. Later that day, Taya posted a note to Chris on Facebook: "Chris, you are the love of my life. You live on in my heart. You always will. I hope we all live lives that make you proud. And babe, rest assured you don't need a fancy resting place—you live on. . . . Safe in the hearts you left behind."[9]

Taya intends to keep Kyle's legacy alive even now that he is gone.

CHAPTER
NINE

A SNIPER'S COMPLICATED LEGACY

A lot happened in the two years after Kyle's murder. Routh went to jail to serve a life sentence. Kyle's second book, *American Gun: A History of the U.S. in Ten Firearms*, was published in 2013 in hardcover and 2014 in paperback to critical acclaim. And sales of *American Sniper*, the proceeds from which are donated to charity and wounded veterans' families, were breaking records. It sold 1.2 million books among all formats (hardcover, paper, and e-book) in 2012 and 2013 and more than 700,000 copies in 2014 and the first months of 2015.[1] Judging from its place at the top of both the *New York Times* and *USA Today* best seller lists, Kyle's autobiography flew off the shelves.

On January 16, 2015, a movie based on Kyle's life, directed by Clint Eastwood and starring Bradley Cooper

Kyle signs a copy of his book *American Sniper* for a fellow serviceman.

(as Chris) and Sienna Miller (as Taya), was released nationwide to captivated audiences. Breaking box office records, *American Sniper* earned $90.2 million on opening weekend in domestic sales and grossed more than $534 million worldwide by the end of March.[2] It was also nominated for six Academy Awards, including Best Motion Picture of the Year and Best Performance

FACT OR FICTION

Clint Eastwood's film *American Sniper* was based on Kyle's autobiography. But as with many book-to-movie translations, not everything in the movie is factually accurate, with events condensed or altered in the interest of time. Here are a few of the differences:

Kyle enlisted in the military because it was a childhood dream, not because of a reaction to the terrorist attacks on September 11, 2001.

The Kyles' wedding was not interrupted by news that the United States was going to war; Chris already knew about his deployment when he and Taya got married.

Chris did call Taya during battle and Taya did overhear a few battle scenes, but not when she called to tell Chris the gender of their first child.

In the opening scene when Kyle makes his first shot as a sniper, he shoots a child. In the book, he shoots a woman, not a child, and does not feel any remorse.

In the film, Ryan Job dies in action; in reality, he survived his injuries and lived for years before dying from complications during facial reconstruction surgery recovery.

The film claims the bounty on Kyle's head was $180,000. In the book, the figure is approximately $20,000–$80,000.[3]

Bradley Cooper played the role of Kyle in the film version of *American Sniper*.

by an Actor in a Leading Role (Bradley Cooper), and won the Oscar for Best Achievement in Sound Editing.[4]

"The movie has become a cultural phenomenon," said Dan Fellman, Warner Bros. head of domestic distribution. "It tore apart the record book and not by a little. By an enormous amount."[5]

Despite Kyle's fame, the former Navy SEAL leaves behind a complicated legacy. He holds the record for the most confirmed and officially documented sniper kills at 160. And he was given multiple awards for his bravery and skill during battle—two Silver Stars, the nation's third highest military decoration; five Bronze Stars for Combat Valor; a Navy and Marine Corps Commendation Medal; and two Navy and Marine Corps Achievement Medals.[6] But demons in Kyle's past have attracted controversy.

Truth or Lies?

It is well known that a career as a decorated military sniper involves killing enemies and violence. But Kyle was often criticized by members of the media and even his readers for showing no remorse for the deaths, particularly those of Iraqis. When asked how many people he killed, he would reply that the exact number did not matter. "I only wish I had killed more," he wrote in *American Sniper*. "Not for bragging rights, but because I believe the world is a better place without savages out there taking American lives."[7]

Kyle has also been accused of stretching the truth during interviews and in his autobiography—mostly when telling stories that involve honor or excessive acts of violence. Kyle claimed that in 2010 when he pulled into a gas station outside Fort Worth, Texas, driving his shiny black F-350 truck, two men approached him and tried to rob him. Kyle said he pulled out a revolver and shot them both dead. Years later, police in the area say they have no record of the assault. But are they merely protecting a former member of the US military?

TERROR IN NEW ORLEANS

Kyle was known for telling outlandish stories, especially in bars. In one particularly horrific account, he claimed he and another SEAL sniper traveled to New Orleans, Louisiana, after Hurricane Katrina to help restore order. According to Kyle, his friend and he went to the top of the Superdome and set up their sniper rifles. Then they shot dozens of people who had armed themselves in case of violence. Was the story true? A spokesman for US Special Operations Command (SOCOM) told a *New Yorker* reporter, "To the best of anyone's knowledge at SOCOM, there were no West Coast SEALs deployed to Katrina."[8]

Kyle appeared on *The Opie & Anthony Show* in January 2012 to promote *American Sniper*. He entertained the hosts with a story about the time he and a few friends went to a bar in Coronado, California, in 2006 after the wake of a Navy SEAL. Many other SEALs and their family members were also at the bar, as was former pro wrestler and one-term Minnesota governor, Jesse Ventura. According to Kyle, "Scruff Face" (i.e., Ventura)—a one-time member of the Underwater Demolition Teams (a predecessor of the SEALs)—loudly voiced his objections to the Iraq War and said the SEALs deserved to "lose a few guys."[9] Kyle told the hosts of *The Opie & Anthony Show* that he punched Ventura and knocked him down.

Did the events in the bar happen the way Kyle said they did? Or was he just prone to embellishing stories for maximum effect? In the years since his death, the "truth" has become harder and harder to verify.

Honor the Soldier

Despite inconsistencies in Kyle's stories, Kyle served his country honorably and made his loved ones proud. When he stopped his excessive drinking and focused more on his family, he became a better husband and good parent to his children. And he was a role model for thousands of veterans—from the Iraq War and others. He worked tirelessly to help them get the physical and emotional support they deserved.

Taya Kyle promises to carry forth her husband's legacy. In March 2015, she announced plans to publish her own memoir on May 4. *American Wife: A Memoir of Love, War, Faith and Renewal* is an intimate account of her relationship with her husband and includes more details about her request for him to leave the military and how she managed raising two toddlers on her own. Her book is not the first tribute to be published about Chris and it certainly will not be the last.

Chris Kyle died an untimely death at the hand of a suffering fellow veteran he attempted to help. But his memory will live on. In the words of his friend and

Kyle's legacy as a heroic US Navy SEAL will live on for years to come.

fellow Navy SEAL, Marcus Luttrell, "A master sniper, Chris has done and seen things that will be talked about for generations to come."[12]

"[Chris] made the decision to get out and be with our family, and looking back now I don't think I ever realized how painful of a decision that was for him. He saw himself as a guardian angel. He didn't care about the number of kills. He cared about the number of lives he saved."[13]

—Taya Kyle

TIMELINE

1974
Christopher Scott Kyle is born on
April 8 in Odessa, Texas.

1992
Kyle graduates from Midlothian High School
and attends Tarleton State University.

1993
Kyle is critically injured in a rodeo
event, ending his rodeo career.

1994
Kyle drops out of college to ranch full time.

1996
Following his dream to join the military, Kyle visits a
recruitment center to enlist. He is rejected because
of the pins in his wrists and returns to ranching.

1999

A call from a navy recruitment officer spurs Kyle to enroll in the BUD/S training course to become a Navy SEAL.

2001

Kyle graduates from BUD/S and is assigned to Navy SEAL Team 3.

2002

Taya and Chris are married on March 16.

2002

Kyle deploys to Kuwait in September.

2003

Saddam Hussein is ousted from power on April 9; he is captured in Tikrit on December 13.

2004

On November 7, Kyle reports for his second tour of duty in Fallujah, Iraq, as an officially trained sniper, just weeks after his son Colton is born.

TIMELINE

2005
Free elections are held in Iraq on January 30 for the first time in 50 years. A parliament is elected on December 15.

2006
Kyle deploys to Ramadi on April 6, only two days after his daughter, McKenna, is born.

2006
Ryan Job is injured on August 2; later that day, Marc Lee becomes the first Navy SEAL to die in combat during the Iraq War.

2008
Kyle reports to Sadr City—his fourth and final tour in Iraq—in April; he returns home in August.

2009
The Kyles relocate to Midlothian, Texas, and Chris becomes the cofounder of Craft International.

2011

Kyle helps form the FITCO Cares Foundation, a nonprofit organization dedicated to helping disabled veterans.

2012

American Sniper, Kyle's memoir about becoming a Navy SEAL, is published on January 3 and becomes a best seller.

2013

Chris Kyle and Chad Littlefield are shot by Eddie Ray Routh at Rough Creek Lodge and pronounced dead on February 2.

2015

American Sniper, the film based on Kyle's life, premieres on January 16.

2015

Eddie Ray Routh's trial begins on February 11. Two weeks later, he is convicted of murdering Kyle and Littlefield and sentenced to life in prison without parole.

ESSENTIAL FACTS

Date of Birth
April 8, 1974

Place of Birth
Odessa, Texas

Date of Death
February 2, 2013

Parents
Wayne and Deby Kyle

Education
Midlothian High School
Tarleton State University

Marriage
Taya Kyle (2002–2013)

Children
Colton Kyle
McKenna Kyle

Career Highlights
From 1999 to 2009, Kyle recorded the most officially documented sniper kills in US military history. He was awarded two Silver Stars, five Bronze Stars, a Navy and Marine Corps Commendation Medal, and two Navy and

Marine Corps Achievement Medals. He is also the published author of one best-selling autobiography, *American Sniper*, and a nonfiction book, *American Gun: A History of the U.S. in Ten Firearms*, and he is the subject of the box office megahit *American Sniper*, directed by Clint Eastwood and starring Bradley Cooper.

Societal Contribution

Following his career as a Navy SEAL sniper and four tours in Iraq, Kyle dedicated his life to helping wounded veterans in the United States. In 2011, he created FITCO Cares Foundation, a nonprofit organization that supplies war veterans with exercise equipment and rehabilitation programs. He also volunteered for the Lone Survivor Foundation and Troops.

Conflicts

When Chris was in the throes of combat, he often neglected his wife and children to focus on his career. Despite Taya's wishes for him to stay in the United States, he reenlisted and served four tours in Iraq. Many controversies surround Kyle's legacy, including stories of messy bar fights and ruthless slayings. Some say Kyle had a volatile temper.

Quote

"I wanted to defend my country, do my duty, and do my job. I wanted, more than anything, to experience the thrill of battle." —*Chris Kyle*

GLOSSARY

bounty
An amount of money given to someone as a reward for catching a criminal.

deploy
To organize and send out people or units to be used for a particular purpose in military service.

insurgent
A person who fights against an established government or authority.

Islam
The religious faith of Muslims including belief in Allah as the sole deity and in Muhammad as his prophet.

jihadist
A Muslim who participates in a holy war on behalf of Islam.

mosque
A building used for Muslim religious services.

Muslim
A person whose religion is Islam.

oust
To remove from property or position by legal action or force.

parliament

The group of people who are responsible for making laws in some governments.

parole

A conditional release of a prisoner serving an indeterminate or unexpired sentence.

Shia (Shiite)

One of the two main branches of Islam that rejects the first three Sunni spiritual leaders and regards Ali, the fourth caliph, as Muhammad's true successor.

sniper

A specially trained and equipped person who shoots at exposed individuals—enemy forces or leaders—from a concealed vantage point or long range.

Sunni

One of the two main branches of Islam, commonly described as orthodox, who believe the leader of Islam should be appointed by election and consensus.

terrorism

The use of violent acts to frighten the people in an area as a way of trying to achieve a political goal.

ADDITIONAL RESOURCES

Selected Bibliography

Kyle, Chris, and Scott McEwen. *American Sniper: The Autobiography of the Most Lethal Sniper in U.S. Military History*. New York: W. Morrow, 2012. Print.

Mooney, Michael J. "The Legend of Chris Kyle." *D Magazine*. D Magazine Partners, Apr. 2013. Web. 2 June 2015.

Schmidle, Nicholas. "In the Crosshairs." *New Yorker*. Condé Nast, 3 June 2013. Web. 2 June 2015.

Further Readings

Lüsted, Marcia Amidon. *The Capture and Killing of Osama Bin Laden*. Minneapolis: Abdo, 2012. Print.

Rowell, Rebecca. *Iraq*. Minneapolis: Abdo, 2012. Print.

Wasdin, Howard E. *I Am a SEAL Team Six Warrior: Memoirs of an American Soldier*. New York: St. Martin's Griffin, 2012. Print.

Websites

To learn more about Essential Lives, visit **booklinks.abdopublishing.com**. These links are routinely monitored and updated to provide the most current information available.

Places to Visit

Islamic Heritage Museum
2315 Martin Luther King, Jr. Ave SE
Washington, DC 10007
202-610-0586
http://www.muslimsinamerica.org
Embrace religious tolerance and learn about the United
States' rich Islamic heritage through rotating exhibits, short
plays, and cultural performances.

The National Navy SEAL Museum and Memorial
3300 N Hwy A1A
Fort Pierce, FL 34949
772-595-5845
https://www.navysealmuseum.org
Visit the only museum dedicated exclusively to preserving
the history of the Navy SEALs and their predecessors.

Rough Creek Lodge and Resort
5165 County Road 2013
Iredell, TX 76649
254-965-3700
http://www.roughcreek.com
Explore Rough Creek Lodge on a hike or in a canoe, go
horseback riding or zoom across the zip line, or play a
competitive game of foosball.

SOURCE NOTES

Chapter 1. Shots Fired

1. Nicholas Schmidle. "In the Crosshairs." *New Yorker.* Condé Nast, 3 June 2013. Web. 2 June 2015.

2. Dan Lamothe. "The Fatal Intersection of Navy SEAL Chris Kyle and the Marine Veteran Who Killed Him." *Washington Post.* The Washington Post Company, 13 Feb. 2015. Web. 2 June 2015.

3. Jordan Breal. "Rough Creek Lodge." *Texas Monthly.* Emmis Publishing, Aug. 2010. Web. 2 June 2015.

4. Melody McDonald Lanier. "Ranger Testifies Killings at Gun Range Were 'Brutal.'" *Statesman.* Cox Media Group, 16 Feb. 2015. Web. 2 June 2015.

Chapter 2. A Texas Cowboy

1. Chris Kyle and Scott McEwen. *American Sniper: The Autobiography of the Most Lethal Sniper in U.S. Military History.* New York: W. Morrow, 2012. Print. 10.

2. Ibid. 13.

3. Ibid. 17.

4. Ibid. 18.

5. Ibid. 18.

6. "U.S. Army Weight Requirements." *Military.com.* Military Advantage, 2015. Web. 2 June 2015.

7. Chris Kyle and Scott McEwen. *American Sniper: The Autobiography of the Most Lethal Sniper in U.S. Military History.* New York: W. Morrow, 2012. Print. 22.

Chapter 3. Training to Become a Hero

1. Chris Kyle and Scott McEwen. *American Sniper: The Autobiography of the Most Lethal Sniper in U.S. Military History.* New York: W. Morrow, 2012. Print. 25.

2. Ibid. 27.

3. Ibid. 26.

4. Alan Duke. "Chris Kyle, America's Deadliest Sniper, Offered No Regrets." *CNN.* Cable News Network, 25 Feb. 2015. Web. 4 June 2015.

5. Stew Smith. "Top 10 Things to Know Before BUD/S." *Military.com.* Military Advantage, 2015. Web. 2 June 2015.

6. Chris Kyle and Scott McEwen. *American Sniper: The Autobiography of the Most Lethal Sniper in U.S. Military History.* New York: W. Morrow, 2012. Print. 33.

7. "Hell Week." *NavySeals.com.* Force12 Media, 2015. Web. 2 June 2015.

8. Chris Kyle and Scott McEwen. *American Sniper: The Autobiography of the Most Lethal Sniper in U.S. Military History.* New York: W. Morrow, 2012. Print. 82.

9. Ibid. 45.

Chapter 4. A Chance Encounter

1. Chris Kyle and Scott McEwen. *American Sniper: The Autobiography of the Most Lethal Sniper in U.S. Military History.* New York: W. Morrow, 2012. Print. 46.

2. Ibid. 49.

3. Ibid. 48.

4. Ibid. 51.

5. "FAQ about 9/11." *9/11 Memorial.* National September 11 Memorial & Museum, 2014. Web. 2 June 2015.

6. Chris Kyle and Scott McEwen. *American Sniper: The Autobiography of the Most Lethal Sniper in U.S. Military History.* New York: W. Morrow, 2012. Print. 60.

7. Chris Spargo. "'I Will Remind You Who You Are When You Forget': American Sniper's Widow Reveals Her Husband's Touching Vows and the Words He Inscribed Inside Her Wedding Ring." *Daily Mail.com.* Associated Newspapers, 28 Jan. 2015. Web. 2 June 2015.

8. Chris Kyle and Scott McEwen. *American Sniper: The Autobiography of the Most Lethal Sniper in U.S. Military History.* New York: W. Morrow, 2012. Print. 60.

Chapter 5. The United States Goes to War

1. "U.S. Launches Cruise Missiles at Saddam." *CNN.com.* Cable News Network, 20 Mar. 2003. Web. 2 June 2015.

2. Chris Kyle and Scott McEwen. *American Sniper: The Autobiography of the Most Lethal Sniper in U.S. Military History.* New York: W. Morrow, 2012. Print. 84.

3. Bryan Long. "Bush: 'No Outcome Except Victory.'" *CNN.com.* Cable News Network, 20 Mar. 2003. Web. 2 June 2015.

4. Chris Kyle and Scott McEwen. *American Sniper: The Autobiography of the Most Lethal Sniper in U.S. Military History.* New York: W. Morrow, 2012. Print. 88.

5. "Jessica Lynch Biography." *Bio.com.* A&E Television Networks, 2015. Web. 2 June 2015.

6. Chris Kyle and Scott McEwen. *American Sniper: The Autobiography of the Most Lethal Sniper in U.S. Military History.* New York: W. Morrow, 2012. Print. 3.

7. Ibid. 4.

8. Ibid. 134, 230.

Chapter 6. Tours of Duty

1. Chris Kyle and Scott McEwen. *American Sniper: The Autobiography of the Most Lethal Sniper in U.S. Military History.* New York: W. Morrow, 2012. Print. 196.

2. "Saddam Hussein Arrested in Iraq." *BBC News.* British Broadcasting Corporation, 14 Dec. 2003. Web. 2 June 2015.

3. Ibid.

4. Chris Kyle and Scott McEwen. *American Sniper: The Autobiography of the Most Lethal Sniper in U.S. Military History.* New York: W. Morrow, 2012. Print. 154.

5. Ibid. 160.

6. Susan Murphy. "10 Years After Battle For Fallujah, Marines Reflect on 'Iconic Fight.'" *NPR.* NPR, 7 Nov. 2014. Web. 2 June 2015.

7. Chris Kyle and Scott McEwen. *American Sniper: The Autobiography of the Most Lethal Sniper in U.S. Military History.* New York: W. Morrow, 2012. Print. 251.

SOURCE NOTES CONTINUED

8. Dexter Filkins. "Defying Threats, Millions of Iraqis Flock to Polls." *New York Times.* The New York Times Company, 31 Jan. 2005. Web. 2 June 2015.

9. Ibid.

10. Ibid.

11. Chris Kyle and Scott McEwen. *American Sniper: The Autobiography of the Most Lethal Sniper in U.S. Military History.* New York: W. Morrow, 2012. Print. 316.

12. Ibid. 345.

Chapter 7. Return to Civilian Life

1. Nicholas Schmidle. "In the Crosshairs." *New Yorker.* Condé Nast, 3 June 2013. Web. 2 June 2015.

2. Chris Kyle and Scott McEwen. *American Sniper: The Autobiography of the Most Lethal Sniper in U.S. Military History.* New York: W. Morrow, 2012. Print. 243.

3. Michael J. Mooney. "The Legend of Chris Kyle." *D Magazine.* D Magazine Partners, Apr. 2013. Web. 2 June 2015.

4. Chris Kyle and Scott McEwen. *American Sniper: The Autobiography of the Most Lethal Sniper in U.S. Military History.* New York: W. Morrow, 2012. Print. 366.

5. Ibid. 422.

6. "Private Military Contractors Under Suspicion for Boston Bombing." *Before It's News.* Before It's News, 18 Apr. 2003. Web. 2 June 2015.

7. Chris Kyle and Scott McEwen. *American Sniper: The Autobiography of the Most Lethal Sniper in U.S. Military History.* New York: W. Morrow, 2012. Print. 424.

8. Jay Langston. "FITCO Cares." *Tactical-Life.* Harris Publications, 1 Mar. 2013. Web. 2 June 2015.

9. Schuyler Kropf. "'American Sniper' Co-Author on Chris Kyle and Putting the Mission into Words." *The Post and Courier.* Evening Post Industries, 28 Mar. 2015. Web. 2 June 2015.

10. Ibid.

11. Chris Kyle and Scott McEwen. *American Sniper: The Autobiography of the Most Lethal Sniper in U.S. Military History.* New York: W. Morrow, 2012. Print. 428.

Chapter 8. Murdered in Cold Blood

1. Nicholas Schmidle. "In the Crosshairs." *New Yorker.* Condé Nast, 3 June 2013. Web. 2 June 2015.

2. Taylor Marsh. "Eastwood's Brooding 'American Sniper' Portrait $90M Box Office Smash." *Taylor Marsh.* Taylor Marsh, 19 Jan. 2015. Web. 2 June 2015.

3. "How Common Is PTSD?" *US Department of Veterans Affairs.* US Department of Veterans Affairs, 10 Nov. 2014. Web. 2 June 2015.

4. Jeff Mosier. "Final Salute: Thousands Pay Respects to Chris Kyle at Cowboys Stadium." *Dallas Morning News.* Dallas Morning News, 12 Feb. 2013. Web. 2 June 2015.

5. Ibid.

6. Ben Russell, Kendra Lynn, and Lindsay Wilcox. "Chris Kyle Funeral Procession Arrives in Austin." *NBCDFW.com.* NBCUniversal Media, 12 Feb. 2013. Web. 2 June 2015.

7. Manny Fernandez and Kathryn Jones. "'American Sniper' Jury Is Told of Troubled Ex-Marine Who Killed Chris Kyle." *New York Times.* New York Times Company, 11 Feb. 2015. Web. 2 June 2015.

8. Michael J. Mooney. "The Legend of Chris Kyle." *D Magazine.* D Magazine Partners, Apr. 2013. Web. 2 June 2015.

9. Phil Hesel. "Widow of 'American Sniper' Chris Kyle Says He'll 'Live On in My Heart.'" *NBCNews.* NBCNews.com, 25 Feb. 2015. Web. 2 June 2015.

10. Nicholas Schmidle. "In the Crosshairs." *New Yorker.* Condé Nast, 3 June 2013. Web. 2 June 2015.

Chapter 9. A Sniper's Complicated Legacy

1. Andy Lewis. "'American Sniper' Book Sales See Continued Bump from Movie's Success." *Hollywood Reporter.* Hollywood Reporter, 6 Feb. 2015. Web. 2 June 2015.

2. "American Sniper." *Box Office Mojo.* IMDb.com, 1 June 2015. Web. 2 June 2015.

3. Courtney Duckworth. "How Accurate Is American Sniper?" *Slate.* The Slate Group, 23 Jan. 2015. Web. 2 June 2015.

4. "Awards." *IMDb.* IMDb.com, 2015. Web. 3 June 2015.

5. Brent Lang. "Box Office: 'American Sniper' Shatters Records With $90.2 Million Weekend." *Variety.* Variety Media, 18 Jan. 2015. Web. 3 June 2015.

6. Lindsay Deutsch. "The Fascinating Life of Chris Kyle, the 'American Sniper.'" *USA Today.* Gannett Company, 23 Jan. 2015. Web. 3 June 2015.

7. Chris Kyle and Scott McEwen. *American Sniper: The Autobiography of the Most Lethal Sniper in U.S. Military History.* New York: W. Morrow, 2012. Print. 5.

8. Nicholas Schmidle. "In the Crosshairs." *New Yorker.* Condé Nast, 3 June 2013. Web. 2 June 2015.

9. Ibid.

10. Mark Joseph Stern. "American Liar." *Slate.* The Slate Group, 20 Jan. 2015. Web. 3 June 2015.

11. Lindsay Deutsch. "The Fascinating Life of Chris Kyle, the 'American Sniper.'" *USA Today.* Gannett Company, 23 Jan. 2015. Web. 3 June 2015.

12. Chris Kyle and Scott McEwen. *American Sniper: The Autobiography of the Most Lethal Sniper in U.S. Military History.* New York: W. Morrow, 2012. Print. Back cover.

13. Douglas Ernst. "'American Sniper' Widow to Release Memoir in May." *Washington Times.* Washington Times, 10 Mar. 2015. Web. 3 June 2015.

INDEX

ABOUT THE AUTHOR

Alexis Burling has written dozens of articles and books for young readers on a variety of topics including current events and famous people, nutrition and fitness, careers and money management, relationships, and cooking. She is also a book critic (and obsessive reader!) with reviews of both adult and young adult books, author interviews, and other publishing industry-related articles published in *The New York Times*, *The Washington Post*, *Chicago Tribune*, and more.